GW00692000

BOOB
Juggling

Written by De-ann Black and the Top That! team
Illustrated by Jools Faiers

KUDOS

Published by Top That! Publishing plc
Tide Mill Way, Woodbridge, Suffolk, IP12 IAP, UK
www.kudosbooks.com
Copyright © 2003 Top That! Publishing plc
Kudos is a Trademark of Top That! Publishing plc

CONTENTS

introduction

Juggling boobs is an activity that almost anyone can be good at – it's an activity where practice really does make perfect. What's more, it is a very good method of relaxing and can help get rid of stress.

The first thing to remember when learning to juggle is to accept that you will drop the boobs many times. Keeping this thought in mind will help to keep frustration at bay and so make mastering the art a speedier and more enjoyable process. It's a good idea to throw the boobs in the air and then let them deliberately land on the floor before you start to practise.

It may sound obvious but you also need to remember to set aside a space for juggling boobs. This will help to ensure that you don't break any family heirlooms.

TROUBLE tumbles

Here are some of the basic juggling technique troubles and common problems – and how to solve them.

FUMBLING

The boobs seem to have a mind of their own. You tend to panic trying to throw and catch at the same time. You probably throw the first boob well, and then your brain goes bananas, panicking about how you're going to catch it and throw another at the same time.

The answer is to slow right down. Fumbling is caused by trying to grab and throw too quickly. Concentrate on each move – and slow down!

RUNNING

You're exhausted running back and forth while juggling. This happens when you throw the boobs too far in front of you.

To stop yourself throwing the boob too far in front of you, stand facing a wall while you practise.

RAGGEDNESS

Raggedness is a common problem. The throws are ragged, the catches are ragged – even your movements are ragged.

You can alleviate this problem by controlling your breathing. If this doesn't do the trick, slow everything down and concentrate on keeping your balance.

WIBBLING

When everything goes haywire, you're wibbling. The boobs fly off in weird directions and nothing you do seems to work.

Wibbling is actually a good sign. It actually suggests that your boob juggling skills are coming together. The wibbling will disappear and soon you'll be juggling boobs brilliantly!

5

WARMING up your BOOBS

Warm up by playing around with the juggling boobs. As with most new activities, juggling will feel awkward to begin with – but take heart, within fifteen minutes you'll start to learn some of the basic moves.

WHERE to JUGGLE?

Juggle wherever there's a space big enough and where you can be confident you won't break anything. If you mind people seeing you make a fool of yourself don't practise in public!

A **GLOSSARY** of JUGLING **Terms**

These words are commonly found in juggling, so it's worth knowing what they mean.

DROPS

As you might expect, this refers to when you drop the boobs.

TOSS

This is the throwing of a boob in an easy arc into the air. Toss it as high as your forehead and as wide as your body. (Scoop tossing refers to tossing the boob in a scooping motion.)

EXCHANGE

This term refers to tossing one boob, then catching another boob using the same hand. Exchanging one boob for another repeatedly is really the key to juggling.

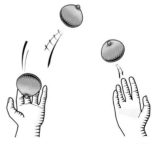

JUGGLING with *ONE* **BOOB**

Don't get ahead of yourself, start with one boob.

1. Stand with your feet shoulder width apart. Stand relaxed. Your arms should be bent to waist level, with palms facing up. This is known as the starting position.

2. Hold one boob in the palm of your dominant hand – your right hand if you are right-handed, your left if you are left-handed. Do not hold the boob on your fingers – hold it in the centre of the palm. This is a basic key to boob juggling.

3. Toss the boob in an arc to your left hand. Use a scooping motion to toss the boob. Toss it as high as your forehead in an arc and catch it in your left hand. Don't raise your left hand to catch the boob. Let it drop down into your hand. Catch it in the palm of your hand.

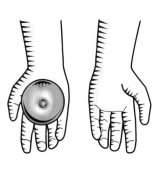

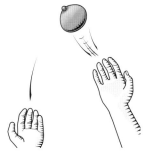

4. Now toss it from your left hand in an arc to your right hand. When you toss the boob, throw it from your palm – don't let it roll off your fingertips. This makes the boob more difficult to control, so use your palm to scoop toss and catch. This makes all the difference when learning how to juggle boobs.

5. Continue tossing it back and forth from one hand to the other. Do this for fifteen minutes, or until you've learned to toss it without it disappearing in all directions.

JUGGLING **TIP**

Tossing the boob correctly is vital! Concentrate on tossing well, rather than catching well. Once you've learned to toss well, catching will follow easily.

JUGGLING with *TWO* **BOOBS**

Are you ready for a pair of boobs!

1. Stand in the starting position. Hold one boob in each palm – palms up.

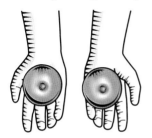

2. Toss one boob up and over to your other hand, using the same arc as before. As the boob reaches the top of its arc and starts to drop down into your other hand (which is holding the second boob), toss the second boob. This is known as the boob exchange.

11

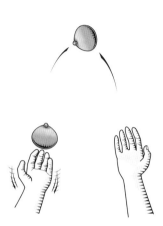

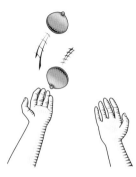

3. Toss the second boob just before you catch the first boob. The boobs will have changed hands – if you've managed to toss and catch them both.

JUGGLING **TIP**

Don't pass the second boob from one hand to the other. You should use a scoop toss for each boob you throw. Each boob must be tossed in the same arc, in other words, scoop tossed at the same height.

CASCADE
(JUGGLING with *THREE*
BOOBS)

**Juggling with three boobs (forwards and in reverse)
is more technically known as a boob cascade.**

The three boobs are
thrown from one hand to
the other, back and
forth, with the throws
going under the incoming
catch. All throws are
underthrows. This
means that each throw is
underneath and inside
the throw before it.

The **FORWARD**
CASCADE

1. Stand in the starting
position. Hold one boob
in the palm of your left
hand and two boobs
in the palm of your
right hand.

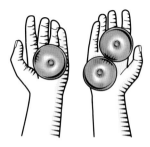

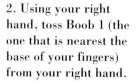

2. Using your right hand, toss Boob 1 (the one that is nearest the base of your fingers) from your right hand.

3. Then toss the boob from your left hand (Boob 2) in the same way as you did when juggling with two boobs.

4. However, before you catch Boob 2 in your right hand, toss Boob 3 in the same arc movement as Boob 1. You should end up with two boobs in your left hand and one boob in your right hand. This is

called a jug. (Two
exchanges back to back
are usually called a jug.)

JUGGLING **TIP**

Always make sure that
the second toss is the
same arc as the first toss.
Don't let the second toss

go across. Remember to
keep your arms bent and
elbows quite close to
your sides (just like in
the starting position).

Clawed CASCADE

The Clawed Cascade uses the same juggling pattern as the normal cascade. The difference is that you catch the boobs with your palms facing downwards – like a claw.

1. Stand in the starting position. Hold one boob in the palm of your left hand and two boobs in the palm of your right hand.

2. Using your right hand, toss Boob 1 (the one that is nearest the base of your fingers) from your right hand.

However, before you catch Boob 2 in your right hand, toss Boob 3 in the same arc movement as Boob 1. You should end up with a pair of boobs in your left hand and one boob in your right hand.

3. Then toss the boob from your left hand (Boob 2) in the same way as you did when juggling with two boobs.

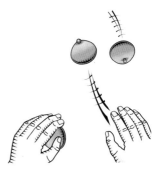

Remember, the pattern of throwing the three boobs is the same as before – but you need to make your tosses and catches with your hand like a claw, facing downwards.

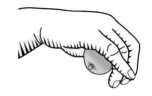

JUGGLING **TIPS**

To practise clawed catches, throw the boob to the opposite hand, and instead of waiting for it to drop in your palm, swing your hand up on the inside of the boob, bring your hand down, and catch it from above.

To practise clawed throws hold one boob with your palm facing down. Gently flick your wrist as you throw the boob upwards in an arc. Catch it, at first, in the opposite hand as usual (with the palm up).

Then practise clawed throws and clawed catches, throwing and catching one boob back and forth.

Reverse CASCADE

When you've mastered the cascade and the clawed cascade, learn the reverse cascade. The moves are basically the same, except they're in reverse.

1. Hold two boobs in your left hand and one in your right. Throw one of the boobs in the left hand in an arc. Once it is over halfway to your other hand, release the boob in your right hand.

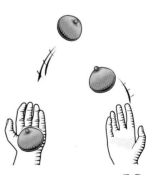

2. Once you have caught the first boob in your right hand and the second boob is halfway to the other hand, throw the third boob up in an arc to the right hand.

3. Keep repeating these moves, remembering that each time a boob reaches the arc, you have to throw another boob over it, making sure they stay on the same path.

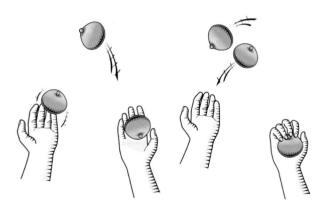

UNDERARM
THROW

Instead of a normal cascade, simply throw one boob under the opposite arm.

1. Begin by standing in the starting position. Take one boob and swing it low and wide underneath the opposite arm.

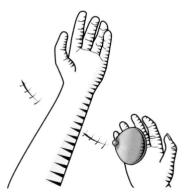

2. Throw the boob so that it rises up in a straight line (to the same height as you would throw in a normal cascade – i.e. forehead level). The boob should fall to a point where you would catch it in a cascade.

JUGGLING **TIP**

Sometimes it helps to make one of your usual scoop tosses higher than usual before you throw the boob underarm. This gives you a little bit more time to toss and catch the boob.

USING THE UNDERARM THROW WHEN PERFORMING A CASCADE

1. Using your right hand, toss Boob 1 (the one that is nearest the base of your fingers) from your right hand.

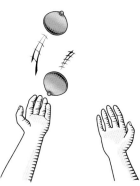

should end up with two
boobs in your left hand
and one boob in your
right hand.

2. Then toss the boob
from your left hand
(Boob 2) in the same way
as you did when juggling
with two boobs.
However, before you
catch Boob 2 in your
right hand, swing Boob 3
low and wide under the
opposite arm. You

Circle JUGGLING

In Circle Juggling the three boobs follow each other in a circular pattern. You must keep two boobs in the air at once.

1. Stand in the starting position, holding two boobs in one hand. One boob should be towards the back of your palm, and one at the base of your fingers. Hold the third boob in your other hand.

2. Toss them both up (one after the other in quick succession) in the same arc, to be caught in the other hand. (Don't toss them up together – toss one slightly before the other in two quick throws.)

3. The third boob is in the opposite hand. Use an underhand throw to exchange the boob into the other hand (the one that has just thrown the two boobs). Then repeat this pattern.

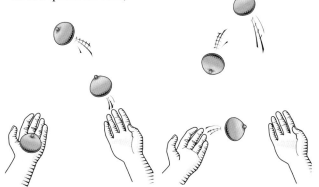

EATING *as YOU JUGGLE your Boobs*

Eating while you juggle boobs can be a lot of fun!

You will need two juggling boobs and one apple. Use an apple that is reasonably small so that you can juggle it easily.

1. Stand in the starting position, holding two boobs in one hand. One boob should be towards the back of your palm, and one at the base of your fingers. Hold the apple in your other hand.

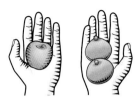

2. Toss both boobs up (one after the other in quick succession) in the same arc, to be caught in the other hand. (Don't toss them up together – toss one slightly before the other in two quick throws.)

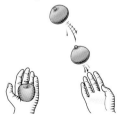

3. The apple is in the opposite hand. Use an underhand throw to exchange the apple into the other hand (the one that has just thrown the two boobs).

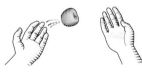

4. Once you're good at this, get ready to take a bite out of the apple.

When you catch one of the boobs in your right hand, and the apple is in your left hand, throw the boob in your right hand higher than you would usually throw it – about a metre higher. By throwing the boob higher, you will give yourself enough time to take a bite out of the apple in your left hand before you throw it up into the air. You have to be quick, but that's part of the fun!

JUGGLING **TIP**

If you want to juggle with three apples, use different coloured ones so that you know which apple you intend to take a bite out of. Bite whichever apple you want, but plan which one you intend to use before you start juggling so you don't get confused!

ARM
bounce

While juggling, bounce the boob in the air off your arm and back into the juggling pattern. This trick is best done as part of a cascade.

1. Stand in the starting position and hold two boobs in one hand, and one in the other.

2. Begin by performing a cascade.

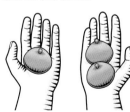

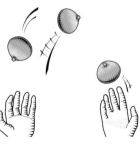

3. Now get ready to bounce one of the boobs off your arm. All you have to do is throw one of the boobs as normal, but instead of catching it in your hand and throwing it up again, let it land on the inside of your arm (near the inside of your elbow or top of your forearm). Then use your arm to knock it back up into the air (as if you had tossed it with your hand). All you're really doing is using your arm to catch and knock the boob back into the juggling pattern.

JUGGLING **TIP**

If you're juggling palms up it's easier to use the inside of your elbow/forearm to knock the boob. But if you're juggling with claw hands use the outside of your elbow/forearm.

30

JUGGLING **boobs** with **ONE HAND**

This is when you keep two boobs in the air with only one hand. Every boob is thrown from the same hand. This is an excellent trick to learn because it helps to improve timing and co-ordination – the vital boob juggling skills.

1. Stand in the starting position, holding two boobs in your dominant hand.

2. Throw one boob up into the air (about as high as your forehead).

throw to the inside of the boob that is dropping down. This will make it look as though the boobs are being thrown in a circular pattern and will stop them colliding.

3. When the boob has reached its highest point, throw the other boob up into the air. Keep your

JUGGLING **TIP**

The key to this trick is practice – and rhythm. Try to control how high you throw the boobs. Keep it the same each time.

4. When you can juggle two boobs, move on and try juggling three. Hold three boobs in your right hand. Throw one up, and when it has almost reached its highest point, throw a second boob up, then throw the third – just in time to catch the first boob! This isn't easy

but is a good exercise to help you improve your boob juggling.

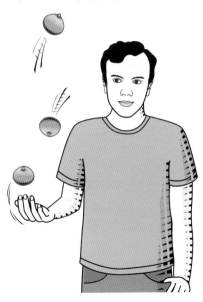

Performing with a **PARTNER**

For this to be successful, you will need a partner who is as good at juggling as you are.

SIDE by **SIDE**

1. Begin by standing side by side in the starting position.

2. Hold one boob each (you'll only need two boobs to begin with). Hold the boobs in your outside hands (the hands that are furthest away from each other).

3. Your partner tosses one boob up in an arc and over to your outside hand.

Your throw needs to go inside their incoming throw (so the boobs don't clash).

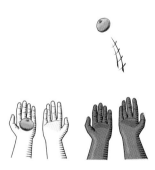

4. You wait until the boob has reached the top of its arc (highest point), then you toss your boob (in an arc) to your partner's outside hand.

5. You catch the incoming boob in your outside hand.

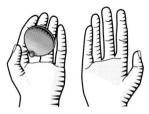

6. Then your partner catches the boob you threw to them in their outside hand. Practise doing this a few times, then change sides, so that you both get a chance to use your other hands as outside hands.

practised – and add the third boob into the juggling (just as you would if you were doing a cascade). Instead of doing one exchange with your partner, you keep going – one exchange follows the other.

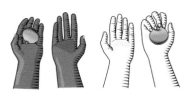

7. Now add the other boob into the performance. Continue doing what you've

FACE to **FACE**

You and your partner will need six juggling boobs for this performance.

1. Stand facing each other a short distance apart. Both of you should be standing in your own starting position. You should be holding two boobs in your right hand and one in your left hand and so should your partner.

2. Each of you starts juggling. Try to begin at the same time. Don't attempt to exchange any boobs at this point. Concentrate on juggling individually but try to keep in time with each other.

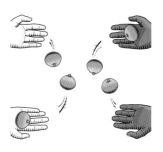

3. Once both of you are juggling three boobs at the same time, be prepared to do your first exchange with each other. On the count of three, toss a boob from your right hand (that would usually be tossed to your own left hand) to your partner's left hand. At the same time, your partner does the same to you.

Make sure the tosses are thrown in an arc to each other (not tossed straight across).

4. After you've made the first exchange, continue juggling individually without doing any exchanges. Juggle for a few moments. This gives you a chance to get in time with each other again.

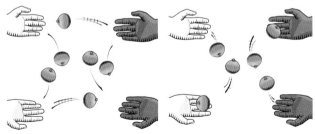

5. When your timing is right, try another exchange – perhaps on the count of three.

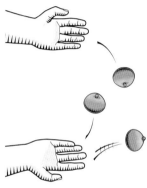

JUGGLING **TIPS**

Obviously this takes lots of practice. What you're aiming for is to exchange boobs and continue juggling. As you get better at this trick, you and your partner will be able to make more exchanges while juggling.

Juggling *with* *CLUBS* and BOOBS

You'll need to improvise for clubs. Why not try a large plastic bottle to start with?

1. Begin by juggling one club and one boob. Toss the club from your left hand to your right hand and the boob from your right hand to your left hand. This will help you to get used to the timing and tosses and releasing the second object. Once you feel comfortable with this movement you can move onto two clubs.

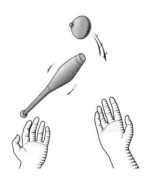

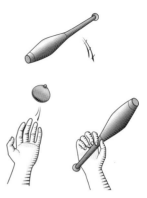

2. To move from two clubs to three, again practise with a boob as the third object. Take a club in each hand and add the boob to your left hand. Try the basic cascade pattern first, starting by tossing the clubs first and finishing off with the boob.

JUGGLING TIP

Remember to wait for each object to peak before you release the next. Take all the moves slowly.

Juggling with THREE **CLUBS** and NO *BOOBS*

If you feel comfortable with two clubs and one boob then try juggling three clubs on their own.

1. Hold two clubs in one hand, with the inner club bulb under the outer. You are going to release the inner one first.

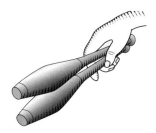

2. Practise releasing the first club and catching it with the other hand. It will be difficult at first, but try to make the tosses consistent.

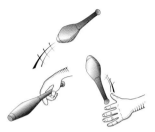

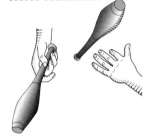

4. Try to keep this pattern going and then take a break. When your throws are accurate, practise more to build up your speed and confidence.

3. Now start with two clubs in one hand and the third in the other. As the first one peaks, launch the second. Repeat this pattern as you launch the third.

43

JUGGLING with **FOOD**

Now try juggling with food!

GO **BANANAS!**

Bananas are ideal for juggling. They look as impressive as boobs to some, don't break easily and the unusual shape makes the movements dazzling.

Use small bananas to begin with and break off any jagged stalks.

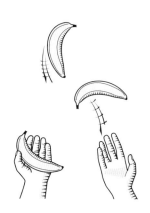

They're a bit difficult to flip properly because of the odd shape, but you'll soon adapt. Try flipping them end-to-end – they'll spin and twirl wonderfully.

TOMATO **TUMBLES**

Firm tomatoes are ideal for juggling. If you drop them too often, they'll fall apart, so be careful not to make a mess.

Choose three red tomatoes, or use red and yellow to add colour.

Tomatoes are best juggled in a cascade.

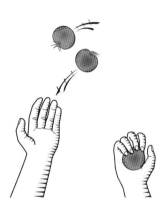

JUGGLING **TIP**

Choose items that are small enough to hold in your hands and make it look fun – that's part of the performance of a true juggler.

Tricky TRICKS
YOU could TRY

When you've mastered the tricks in this book, why not have a go at some of these?

CHOPS

Chops can take months to perfect so patience is required. Start by juggling a three-boob cascade, then choose a boob and quickly carry it over the incoming boob, down to the opposite arm. Then toss it straight up the side. Then you go back and catch the incoming boob. Practise doing this with both hands, and when you can do it well with both hands do both hands together.

BLIND JUGGLING

Blind juggling doesn't involve doing tricks any different to the ones described in this book. It's just with an added difficulty: you wear a blindfold. The only way to master this skill is through hours and hours of practice.

OVERHEAD JUGGLING

Start by lying down on the floor. You use the same technique to juggle overhead as you did when learning to juggle: starting with one boob and working your way up. It's harder because you have to push the boobs up instead of being able to toss them. The patterns are the same but at first your tricep muscles will hurt and you won't be able to practise for long.

Juggling **BOOBS** **ON** the *FLOOR*

Juggling boobs on the floor or sitting down
can also be fun. You could kneel, sit cross-legged,
sit on a chair or bean bags – however you feel
most comfortable.

People don't expect to see boob jugglers sitting
down so if you're willing to perform in public, this
will add an element of surprise to your
performance.

If you can continue juggling boobs as you move
from sitting down to kneeling to standing up, then
you really will be a star!